A Robbie Reader

Meet Our New Student From

MALAYSIA

Ann Weil

Mitchell Lane
PUBLISHERS

P.O. Box 196
Hockessin, Delaware 19707
Visit us on the web: www.mitchelllane.com
Comments? email us: mitchelllane@mitchelllane.com

Meet Our New Student From

Australia • China • Colombia • Great Britain
• Haiti • Israel • Korea • **Malaysia** • Mexico
• New Zealand • Nigeria • Tanzania

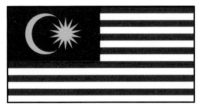

PUBLISHER'S NOTE: The facts on which the story
in this book is based have been thoroughly
researched. Documentation of such research
can be found on page 44. While every possible
effort has been made to ensure accuracy, the
publisher will not assume liability for damages
caused by inaccuracies in the data, and
makes no warranty on the accuracy of the
information contained herein.

To reflect current usage, we have chosen to
use the secular era designations BCE
("before the common era") and CE ("of the
common era") instead of the traditional
designations BC ("before Christ") and AD
(anno Domini, "in the year of the Lord").

ABOUT THE INSECTS: Malaysia is known for its
variety of insects. The following insects are
shown on the running heads of this book:
leaf bug (chapter 1), Rajah Brooke birdwing
butterfly (chapter 2), rhinoceros beetle
(chapter 3), shield bug nymph (chapter 4),
and yellow walking stick (chapter 5).

**Library of Congress Cataloging-in-Publication
Data**

Weil, Ann.
  Meet our new student from Malaysia / by Ann
Weil.
     p. cm. — (Robbie reader)
  Includes bibliographical references and
index.
  ISBN 978-1-58415-654-3 (library bound)
  1. Malaysia—Juvenile literature. I. Title.
DS592.W395 2008
959.5—dc22
                                    2008002811

Printing   1   2   3   4   5   6   7   8   9

                                              PLB

CONTENTS

Malaysia

Kuala Lumpur, the capital of Malaysia, with its skyscrapers and the Petronas Twin Towers (left), is a bustling city with a variety of people, customs, religions, and ethnic groups.

What's in a Name?

Lucy was five minutes late to class. It was pouring rain outside and she was dripping wet. It seemed like it was always raining in Seattle, Washington, in the fall. Lucy was used to the wet weather, but this morning she had forgotten to grab her rain hat as she raced out the door. Water ran through her thick curly hair and down her face. Monday mornings were never easy for her, but this Monday was starting off terribly.

"Sorry," she said to her teacher, Mr. Baker, as she took her seat. She saw he had written *Malaysia* on the blackboard.

"*Selamat pagi,* Lucy," he said. He didn't seem to mind that she was late. But what was he saying? It sounded like *seh-laah-MAHT PAH-gee.*

"That means 'good morning' in Bahasa Malaysia," Mr. Baker explained. "Bahasa Malaysia is the official language of the country we will study this week." He pointed to the word on the board.

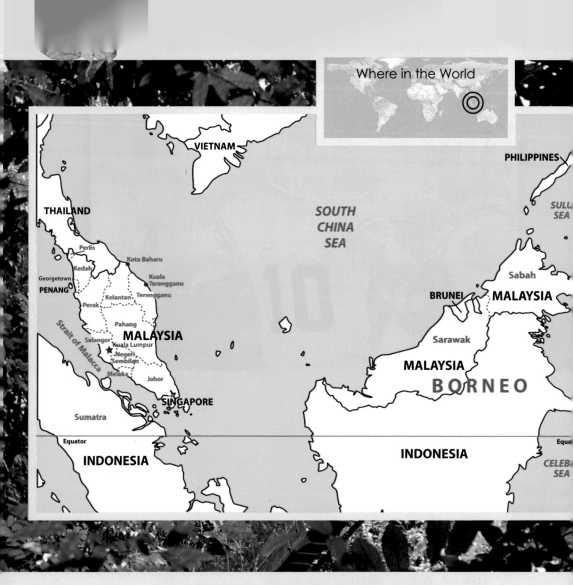

Where in the World

VIETNAM

PHILIPPINES

THAILAND

SOUTH
CHINA
SEA

SULU
SEA

Perlis

Kota Baharu

Kedah

Georgetown

PENANG

Kuala
Terengganu

Perak

Kelantan

Terengganu

Sabah

BRUNEI

MALAYSIA

Pahang

Selangor

MALAYSIA

Kuala Lumpur

Negeri
Sembilan

Sarawak

Strait of Malacca

Melaka

Johor

MALAYSIA

BORNEO

SINGAPORE

Sumatra

Equator

Equa

INDONESIA

INDONESIA

CELEB
SEA

FACTS ABOUT MALAYSIA

Malaysia Total Area:
127,316 square miles
(329,750 square kilometers)

Population:
25,274,133 (2008 estimate)

Capital City:
Kuala Lumpur

Monetary Unit:
Ringgit

Religious Groups:
Islam, Buddhist, Christian, Hindu,
Confucianism, Taoism, and others

Languages:
Bahasa Malaysia (official), English,
Chinese (Cantonese, Mandarin, Hokkien,
Hakka, Hainan, Foochow), Tamil, Telugu,
Malayalam, Punjabi, Thai (in East Malaysia,
Iban, Kadazan and several other
indigenous languages are spoken)

Chief Exports:
Electronic equipment, gas, oil, wood and
wood products, palm oil, rubber, textiles,
chemicals

Already a few hands were raised. Mr. Baker called on Sofia. "Where is Malaysia?" she asked.

Mr. Baker walked over to the large wall map of the world. "Malaysia has two parts. East Malaysia is here, on the island of Borneo, and West Malaysia is here, on a **peninsula** below Thailand." He wrote the word *peninsula* on the board, under *Malaysia*. "*Peninsula* means 'almost an island.' You see how this part of Malaysia is almost surrounded by water? This is why West Malaysia is sometimes called *peninsular Malaysia*."

Lucy opened her notebook to a new page. She wrote *Malaysia* at the top and *peninsula* underneath. She liked learning new words. She listened to Mr. Baker as she wrote. "A new student is joining our class next week, from Malaysia." He wrote *Kim Ling Tan* on the board. "Tan is a common family name among Chinese Malaysians. Chinese Malaysians make up about one-quarter of the people in Malaysia."

"What other names are common in Malaysia?" asked Ben.

Mr. Baker wrote *Ben bin Robert* on the board. "Hey, Robert is my father's name," said Ben.

"Exactly," said Mr. Baker. "Many Malay people do not use last names as we do in America. A child is given a first name, followed by *bin*, which means 'son of,' or *binte*, which means 'daughter of,' and then the father's first name."

"So I am Lucy binte Michael," said Lucy.

Chapter 1

Everyone had a chance to say his or her new name: Jack bin Peter, Sofia binte Paul, Carrie binte Ken . . .

"Very good," said Mr. Baker. "When you see a name like that, you know the person is **Muslim**—although many Muslim people now drop the *bin* and *binte* before their father's name. And within families, people do not even use the first names. They call each other by their position in the family, such as 'father's eldest sister.' "

"So I am 'middle son,' " said Ben.

"You can often tell what group Malaysians belong to by their names," Mr. Baker said. "Each group has different customs. They practice different religions. They wear different clothing styles. They eat different foods. But the groups still get along and socialize, and they share traditions with one another."

"Do they have hamburgers in Malaysia?" asked Lucy. Hamburgers were her favorite food.

"Yes, people eat hamburgers in Malaysia, but they call them beefburgers," said Mr. Baker.

"Why?" asked Ben.

"About half the people of Malaysia are Muslim, and Muslims do not eat pork," said Mr. Baker. "They would not want to eat something they thought might include ham, or any other meat from a pig." All this talk of hamburgers was making Lucy hungry.

"What games do they play in Malaysia?" asked Jack. He loved sports and usually wore a T-shirt with the name of a ball team on it.

"They play a game called *sepak takraw*," said Mr. Baker. He wrote the word on the board. "It's like a cross between volleyball and soccer. Players cannot use their hands or arms to get the ball over the net, which isn't as high as a volleyball net."

"*Seh-pak tak-raw*," Jack pronounced slowly. "I'll have to try that sometime."

Sepak takraw, or kick volleyball, is a popular sport throughout Southeast Asia. It is like volleyball except that players can only touch the ball with their feet, knee, chest, or head. Each team, called a *regu*, has three players. People used to weave the balls themselves using natural materials, such as **rattan**. Now the balls are made of plastic instead.

The bell rang for recess. Lucy looked out the window. The rain had stopped, and the sun was peeking through the clouds. It was turning out to be a fine day after all.

James Brooke speaks with Muda Hassim, the uncle of the sultan of Brunei, in 1842. Brooke was a British army officer before he became the first white rajah of Sarawak.

Woodville. 1902.

A Brief History of
Malaysia

Chapter **2**

Malaysia is a new country. Even the name *Malaysia* is new. It was not used until 1963. Before that, it was called Malaya. Before that, the region had different names and different boundaries, depending on its rulers.

Today, people need special papers, such as a passport, to enter a country. But long ago, the area of Malaysia was one land without borders. To talk of Malaysia throughout history is to talk of a region that included areas that are now part of Indonesia and other countries.

Trading by Sea

In ancient times, travel by sea was easier than travel over land. The Strait of Malacca (muh-LAH-kah) was an important trade route. This narrow body of water connects the South China Sea to the Indian Ocean. Traders from all over Asia, including India, China, Persia (modern-day Iran), and Arabia, sailed up and down the Strait of Malacca. They found good places along this route for their boats to stop and do business. They traded spices, gold, and other goods of value, including sweet-smelling sandalwood.

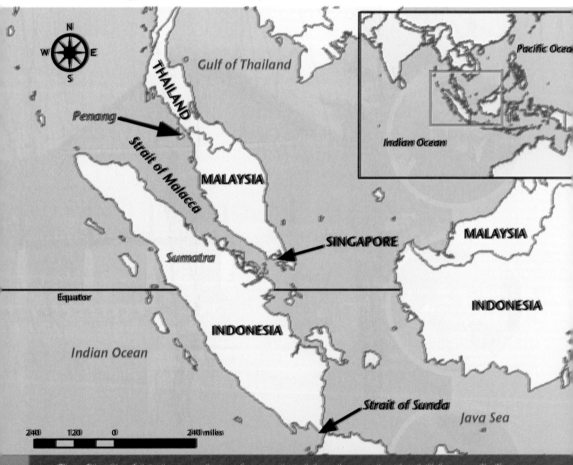

The Strait of Malacca is an important trade route, but this small slice of ocean is not a peaceful place. Throughout history, pirates called lanun (lah-noon) have preyed on ships traveling through the strait. Pirates still threaten ships along this route. They use their small, fast boats to attack ships and hijack them. Then they hide among the tiny islands and in the narrow rivers along the swampy coastline.

Traders also brought their traditions and religions with them. This changed the lives of the people who already lived there. The original people were **animists**. Animists believe that spirits live in natural objects, such as rivers, rocks, and the wind, as well as in living things, including plants and animals. Arab traders were Muslim. They brought the religion of **Islam** to this region.

Over time, these trading ports grew into towns. Some became centers of small empires ruled by a sultan. A sultan is like a king. He would pass his land and power to his son. The sultans were Muslim, and many people converted to their rulers' religion.

Melaka

The port of Melaka (which is also spelled *Malacca*) was the perfect trading port. Its harbor was deep enough for big ships. It was on the trade route, and it was close to Sumatra (soo-MAH-truh), just across the narrow Strait of Malacca.

Portuguese and Dutch traders used the Strait of Malacca, too. A Portuguese fleet invaded Melaka in 1511. If they controlled this port, they would have power over the spice trade. They also wanted to convert the people from Islam to **Christianity**. The Portuguese stayed in power for about a hundred years, but they did not convert many people to their religion. Beginning in 1640, Dutch traders forced the Portuguese out of power.

An engraving, made in the early 1800s, of the port and town of Melaka. Some of the historic buildings still stand. The old fort and church are now ruins.

England had its eye on Melaka as well. Unlike the Portuguese, Dutch traders were not focused on Melaka. They traded more widely throughout the region. In 1824, the Dutch signed over control of Melaka to England. Other parts of the peninsula were already under British rule. The British united Melaka with Penang and Singapore under the name Straits Territories.

Sarawak and Sabah

Sarawak (suh-RAH-wok) is the largest state in present-day Malaysia. It is on the island of Borneo (BOR-nee-oh). Another Malaysian state, Sabah (SAH-bah), is also on Borneo. The early people of Borneo were very different from those who lived on the peninsula. The people of Borneo belonged to many different tribes. Some were headhunters. Borneo was not on the trade route. For these reasons, it developed differently than Melaka.

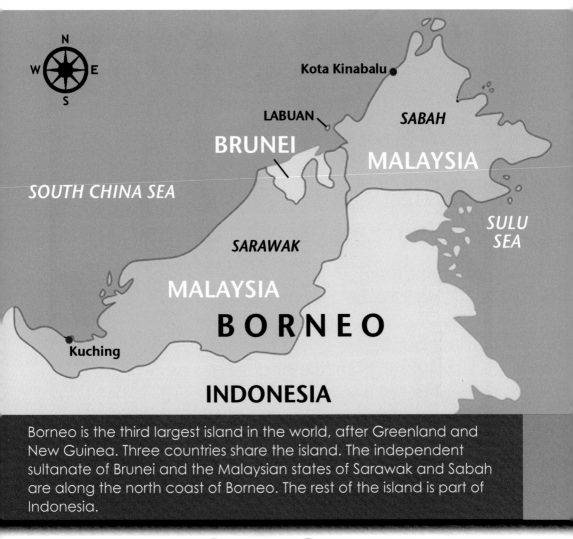

Borneo is the third largest island in the world, after Greenland and New Guinea. Three countries share the island. The independent sultanate of Brunei and the Malaysian states of Sarawak and Sabah are along the north coast of Borneo. The rest of the island is part of Indonesia.

Around 1840, an English adventurer named James Brooke was visiting Sarawak. At that time, Sarawak was under the rule of the Sultan of Brunei (broo-NYE). Brooke helped the **rajah**, or prince, put down a rebellion against the sultan's rule.

The rajah was grateful. Brooke became a rajah himself, and ruled until 1868. He won the people's respect. His nephew Charles Brooke was rajah after James died. Then Charles's son, Charles Vyner Brooke, became the third white rajah of Sarawak. He ruled until Japan invaded in 1941.

Modern History

The Japanese held Borneo and peninsular Malaysia during World War II. After the war, Britain regained control, but it was not a peaceful time. The people did not want British rule and fought back. In 1957, the **Federation** of Malaya gained independence from Britain. In 1963, Sarawak, Sabah, and the island of Singapore on the tip of the peninsula united with Malaya to form a new country with a new name: Malaysia. Two years later, Singapore became an independent country.

Malaysian Government Today

Most Malaysian states are still ruled by sultans. Every five years, one sultan is elected king of Malaysia for a five-year term. Malaysia also has a prime minister and other elected officials in its government.

Mahathir kept a tight control over government. He focused on making Malaysia a wealthy and modern country.

Mahathir bin Mohamad was the prime minister of Malaysia from 1981 to 2003. He was Asia's longest serving elected ruler. Mahathir was a doctor before he became prime minister, and was known as Dr. Mahathir, or simply Dr. M.

The Rafflesia flower can grow to about 40 inches across. Some flowers smell sweet, but the Rafflesia has a strong smell like rotting meat. After five or six days, the flower wilts and the petals turn black.

There are several tea plantations in the Cameron Highlands, where the rain and rich soil make the land ideal for growing many fruit and vegetable crops. Visitors can also see how tea is harvested and processed for use.

A milky liquid, called latex, drips from a tap in this rubber tree. The latex is just behind the bark of the tree. It takes skill to cut the bark so that the latex can drip out, without damaging the tree.

Rubber

Rubber trees are not native to Malaysia. They were brought in from Brazil, in South America. By the end of the 1800s, rubber plantations covered about 7,500 square miles of peninsular Malaysia. Malaysia became the world's biggest rubber producer. This is still an important industry in Malaysia. The country is the third largest rubber producer in the world, after Thailand and Indonesia.

Workers tap the trees by cutting into the bark with a very sharp knife. A milky liquid called latex oozes out and drips into a cup. The cups of latex are emptied into a bigger container, and the latex is treated, rolled, and dried to make rubber.

*fun*FACTS

The name *rubber* came about after someone discovered that it could "rub out," or erase, pencil marks.

Hundreds of years ago, rubber was used to make balls that bounced. This wonderful invention still amuses many people. The soles of some shoes have rubber. Rubber is used to make hoses. Some rugs and carpets have foam rubber underneath. Another important place that rubber is used is in car tires.

A Malay family wears formal clothing for a Hari Raya Puasa feast, which celebrates the end of Ramadan.

People of
Malaysia

Chapter

Malaysia is a nation of different groups of people, with different customs and lifestyles. The country has some of the tallest skyscrapers in the world (the Petronas Twin Towers are 1,483 feet tall), and business people wear suits in the capital city, Kuala Lumpur. Across the South China Sea, in Sarawak, tribal people wear traditional dress.

The United States has been called a "melting pot," because when people moved to America from other countries, they and their children picked up the new customs of their adopted land. This is often not the case in Malaysia. People in Malaysia maintain the traditions of their original lands. They tend to live and marry within their own ethnic groups.

The official language of Malaysia is Bahasa Malaysia, but many Malaysians speak their own language at home and within their groups—such as Mandarin (Chinese) or Tamil.

Chapter 4

Orang Asli

Orang Asli means "original people." The Orang Asli lived on the Malay Peninsula before the Malay people arrived. They were traditionally hunters, farmers, and fishers. Some Orang Asli still live close to nature. They collect fruit and bamboo from the forest to sell.

Sons of the Soil

Malaysians are either Bumiputra (boo-mee-POO-truh) or non-Bumiputra. *Bumiputra* means "son of the soil." Many Bumiputra have ancestors who lived in East or West Malaysia or Indonesia, or traveled back and forth across the sea and the Strait of Malacca. About half the population of Malaysia are Bumiputra.

Indian Muslims are Bumiputra, but Malaysians with ancestors from other places, such as China, are not. They are non-Bumiputra.

Chinese

The Chinese are the largest group of non-Bumiputra. More than a quarter of Malaysians are Chinese. Most live in towns and cities. Many Malaysian shops and businesses are owned and run by Chinese Malaysians, who tend to be better educated and wealthier than Bumiputra.

Chinese Malaysians enjoy food that other Malaysians do not often eat. They make a bird's nest soup from real birds' nests! This kind of nest is made almost entirely from the birds' saliva. The saliva gives the soup its special flavor.

Indian

Although some early traders came from India, most did not stay to live. Malaysian Indians are mostly descended from workers brought in to work on plantations. This ethnic group makes up about 8 percent of the total population of Malaysia. Many of these Indians are **Hindu**. Hindu temples have colorful statues of their gods.

Statues of the Hindu god Ganesha (also called Ganesh) decorate Hindu temples, such as this one in Kuala Lumpur. Ganesha, a popular, important god, has a head like an elephant's and many arms.

Straits Chinese

Some early Chinese traders settled along the Strait of Malacca. They were upper-class merchants and married local Malay women. Over hundreds of years, their culture, called Peranakan (*per-AH-nuh-kahn,* meaning "born here" in the Malay language), grew out of these early mixed marriages. The marriages between these people also produced a marriage of food traditions. Peranakan dishes use Chinese ingredients with Malay spices. Peranakan is considered one of the finest **cuisines** of Malaysia.

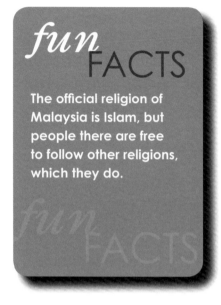

Food Customs

Chinese people eat with chopsticks. They eat many kinds of vegetables and meat, including pork. Muslims do not eat pork. The Muslim custom is to eat with only the right hand, because the left hand is used for attending to matters in the bathroom. Many Hindus do not eat beef, and some are vegetarians. Indian "banana leaf" restaurants serve rice and curries on banana leaves instead of on plates.

Malaysians often eat on the go. They buy meals and snacks from food hawkers and eat them at

outdoor tables. Food hawkers are people who pre-
pare and sell food on city streets. Some cities have
hawker centers, like huge food courts. Food hawkers
serve up dumplings, *nasi goreng* (fried rice), noodle
dishes, grilled meat, ice cream, and cold drinks. Rice
dishes are especially popular, even for breakfast.

Nasi lemak is a rice dish served for breakfast or lunch. Rice cooked
in coconut milk may be served with fried peanuts, a boiled or
scrambled egg, small fried fish, and pickled vegetables.

Holidays and Celebrations

The different ethnic groups in Malaysia have their own special holidays.

Chinese New Year

Chinese New Year is a big celebration among Chinese Malaysians. Chinese merchants burn fake paper money in the streets to bring good luck and good fortune to their businesses. There are traditional Chinese dragon dances in the streets. Red packets of money are passed around as gifts.

Buddhist Chinese Malaysians also observe Wesak Day, which celebrates the birth, teachings, and death of Gautama Buddha.

Indian Festivals

Malaysian Indians celebrate Deepavali (dee-puh-VAH-lee), the festival of light. They also celebrate Thaipusam (TY-poo-sam). For this noisy, exciting festival, thousands of Indian Malaysians walk miles from temples in Kuala Lumpur to the Batu Caves on the outskirts of the city. Some carry honey or milk to honor the Hindu god Lord Murugan. Some walk with metal rods through their cheeks. Others have hooks in their backs. Some carry kavadi (kuh-VAH-dee), which are large colorful structures that are attached to metal hooks that pierce the skin. What is most amazing is that they do not seem to feel pain. They are in a **trance**, and do not bleed.

A Chinese Malaysian girl (above) places coins into a donation pot held by a Buddha statue at a Buddhist temple in Kuala Lumpur on the eve of Wesak Day.

Thaipusam is a holiday with many traditions of celebration. Some people insert hooks with dangling bells and limes through their backs, and others pierce their cheeks and tongues with metal rods.

Satay

Ketupat

Roti canai

Ais kacang

Hari Raya Puasa

For one month each year, called **Ramadan**, Muslim people do not eat anything between sunrise and sunset each day. Hari Raya Puasa celebrates the end of the month of Ramadan. People dress in their best clothes. There are big feasts. A Hari Raya Puasa banquet might include *laksa*, which are noodles with fish curry sauce. Guests can add cucumbers, mint, red peppers, and onions. **Lemang** is sticky rice cooked with coconut milk in **pandan** leaves and steamed or roasted inside bamboo shoots. The pandan leaves have a special fragrance. **Rendang** is made with chicken or beef cooked with spices and coconut milk. **Satay** is tasty chunks of barbecued meat cooked on skewers and dipped in a peanut sauce. **Ketupat** is rice that has been boiled in woven palm leaves; when it is finished cooking, it is pressed together in cubes.

A Hari Raya Puasa feast might also include some Indian foods, such as **roti canai** (flatbread) with **dhal** (sauce made with chick peas), and Indian curries; and Chinese foods such as **mee** (noodles) and **char keoway teow** (fried flat noodles).

There are many cakes and cookies for dessert, including Malay cakes made with rice flour, coconut milk, sugar, and eggs. *Tapai* is a fermented rice pudding made with yeast. A popular treat for children is *ais kacang* (ice kah-CHANG), which is a Malaysian version of shaved ice smothered in colorful syrup, and sometimes topped with jelly or preserves.

Malaysia

Kim Ling's view from the balcony of her house in Penang. The outbuildings were once part of a pig farm, but now they house a restaurant.

Selamat Pagi,
Kim Ling
Chapter

5

Everyone in Lucy's class wanted to share something interesting that they had learned about Malaysia. They spent the day before Kim Ling's first day giving their reports.

Jack gave a report on *sepak takraw*. He showed us how to play the game outside in the school yard.

Ben did his report on kite fighting, a kind of kite-flying competition. "First the kite string is dipped in a soft sticky gum, then in powdered glass," Ben explained. "People try to move their kite string across another person's. The glass will cut their opponent's kite string in midair!"

Lucy did a report on clothing. She wrapped a big silk scarf around her hair and told the class that many Malay girls and women choose to wear the *tudung*, or head scarf. They wrap a big silk scarf tightly over their hair and under their chin.

The class was ready the morning Kim Ling was to arrive.

ENGLISH	BAHASA MALAYSIA
Welcome	Selamat datang
Good morning	Selamat pagi
Good afternoon	Selamat tengahari
Good evening	Selamat petang
Good night	Selamat malam
Goodbye	Selamat Jalan or Selamat Tinggal
Thank you	Terima Kasih
Yes	Ya
No	Tidak (tak)

"*Selamat pagi!*" they said all together when Mr. Baker walked in with Kim Ling.

Even with all that they had learned about Malaysia, the class had many questions for their new student. Mr. Baker asked Kim Ling if she would like to answer some of their questions, and she agreed.

"Do you have brothers and sisters?" asked Sofia.

Kim Ling nodded. "I have two sisters. Their names are Kim Lian and Kim Fang."

"Why do you all have the same first name?" asked Lucy.

"It is a Chinese custom," said Kim Ling.

Mr. Baker explained, "That is how people know the girls are sisters. Boys also have the same first name as their brothers."

"Why did you move here?" asked Ben.

"My uncle and aunt live in Seattle," said Kim Ling. "When my parents got permission to come to America to work, we wanted to live close to family."

Kim Ling showed us some pictures she had taken in Malaysia. She took this photo while she was visiting a butterfly farm. The twins are looking at Rajah Brooke birdwing butterflies on bright pink flowers.

"Where did you live in Malaysia?" asked Carrie.

"My family lived in Penang," Kim Ling answered.

"That's an island," said Jack. He had studied the map of Malaysia. "Do you have to take a boat to get there from the mainland?" he asked.

"There is a bridge for cars and buses," she said.

Kim Ling told the class about her house in Malaysia. Her mother had a restaurant behind their house where there used to be a pig farm. Sometimes Kim

Kim Ling showed us more photos. "Here I am with some school-mates at my school in Penang. I was wearing a tie because I was the class monitor. We are wearing our school uniform. I thought I would have to buy a new uniform for this school, but now I see that will not be necessary."

Ling would help out at the restaurant. "I liked making *laksa*," she said. "It is my favorite food to make and to eat."

"Thank you, Kim Ling," said Mr. Baker, signaling an end to their questions.

Lucy had so many more things to ask, but she knew she would have plenty of time. Her parents had said she could invite Kim Ling and her family over for dinner!

How To Make
Sticky Rice with Mango

Things You Will Need

- An adult
- Bowl
- Saucepan
- Stove
- Spoon
- Pot holder
- Steamer or double saucepan
- Ramekins or small cups
- Plastic wrap

Ingredients

- 2 cups glutinous (sticky) rice, soaked in water for at least one hour and drained
- 1½ cups coconut mik, canned or freshly prepared
- A pinch of salt
- 2 tablespoons of sugar
- 2 large ripe mangoes, peeled and chopped (or sliced strawberries)

Instructions

1. Put the rice, coconut milk, salt, sugar, and 1¼ cup water in a saucepan.
2. With the help of an adult, bring the ingredients to a boil.
3. Stir. Lower the heat and simmer, uncovered, about 8 to 10 minutes until all the liquid is absorbed.
4. Have the adult remove the pan from the heat. Cover and let stand for 5 minutes.
5. Spoon the rice to a steamer or double saucepan.
6. Have an adult steam the rice 15 to 20 minutes over boiling water, until the rice is cooked through.
7. Mold the cooked rice into individual ramekins or small cups lined with plastic wrap. Cool to room temperature.
8. At serving time, lift the rice out and place it on a plate. Top each serving with mango pieces (or sliced strawberries).

Make Your Own
Batik T-Shirt

You Will Need

Pattern

An adult to help you

White t-shirt

Pencil

Elmer's® Glue-All®

Marker

Spray water bottle

Cold water spray fabric dye

Large plastic trash bag

Batik is an ancient art for creating designs on cloth using wax and colorful dyes. It became a tradition on Java, an island of Indonesia, and moved across the Java Sea to Malaysia. Long ago, batik was a hobby among royal women in Southeast Asia. Now people all over the world create beautiful batik designs. So can you!

Instructions for a Batik T-shirt

Traditional batik uses hot wax to create designs.
You will use glue instead.

 1 Use a pencil to sketch a design on a piece of white paper. This way it will be easy to erase and make changes to your pattern. When you are happy with your design, go over your sketch with a dark marker to make it stand out clearly.

 2 Cover a flat work area with a large plastic trash bag. Spread a white cotton T-shirt on the bag. Center the piece of paper with your design inside the shirt. Your pattern will show through the cloth. Use the glue bottle like a pen to follow the outline of your pattern. Fill in the outline with glue. You can scribble the glue to make it look more like batik that is created using wax. Dot the glue around the neckline and sleeves. If you want, add dots of glue over other parts of the T-shirt, too. The places with glue will not pick up the dye. Let the glue dry on the shirt front. Then turn the shirt over and make more glue dots or patterns on the back. Let that glue dry.

 3 When the glue is completely dry, remove the paper pattern from inside the shirt. Hang the shirt on a hanger. Take it outside, if possible, because this next part can get messy. If that is not possible, hang the shirt over the bathtub.

 4 Spray the top half of the shirt with cold water spray fabric dye. Spray the bottom half with plain water. The dye will bleed down into the wet area.

 5 Let the shirt dry, then hand rinse the shirt in cool water to wash away any remaining glue. After you wear your new shirt, you may wash it according to the package directions on the dye.

Further Reading

Books

Allman, Barbara. *The Petronas Towers* (Building World Landmarks). Farmington Hills, Michigan: Blackbirch Press, 2004.

Di Piazza, Francesca. *Malaysia in Pictures* (Visual Geography). Minneapolis, Minnesota: Twenty-First Century Books, 2006.

Heinrichs, Ann. *Malaysia* (True Books). Danbury, Connecticut: Children's Press, 2005.

McNair, Sylvia. *Malaysia* (Enchantment of the World, Second Series). Danbury, Connecticut: Children's Press, 2002.

Munan, Heidi. *Malaysia* (Cultures of the World). Tarrytown, New York: Benchmark Books, 2001.

Pundyk, Grace. *Welcome to Malaysia* (Welcome to My Country). Milwaukee: Gareth Stevens Publishing, 2004.

Works Consulted

This book is based on author Ann Weil's personal experiences in Malaysia. The author also consulted with her Chinese Malaysian friends in Penang for the facts in this book. Other works consulted are listed below.

"Chinese Names," from *China: A Teaching Workbook.* © Columbia University, East Asian Curriculum Project. http://afe.easia.columbia.edu/china/autobio/names.htm

Gwin, Peter. "Dangerous Straits." *National Geographic,* October 2007. http://ngm.nationalgeographic.com/2007/10/malacca-strait-pirates/pirates-text

Hooker, Virginia Matheson. *A Short History of Malaysia*. Crows Nest, NSW, Australia: Allen & Unwin, 2003.

Malaysia and Singapore. New York: DK Travel, 2007.

Malaysian Rubber Board. "The Story of Malaysian Natural Rubber." http://www.lgm.gov.my/general/storymnr.html

Malaysian Timber Council. "Malaysia Has Big Ambitions for Its Rubberwood Industry." August 30, 2004. http://www.mtc.com.my/news/pr175.htm

Trade Environment Database. "Tin Mining in Malaysia." http://www.american.edu/TED/tin.htm

Witham, Lynn. *Kuala Lumpur, Malaysia (Culture Shock! At Your Door: A Survival Guide to Customs and Etiquette)*. Portland, Oregon: Graphic Arts Center Publishing Company, 2004.

Further Reading

Web Sites

The A to Z of Materials: Natural Rubber / Latex—Production of Natural Rubber
http://www.azom.com/details.asp?ArticleID=3580

All About Malaysia
http://www.geocities.com/TheTropics/Shores/3187/

U.S. Department of State: Malaysia
http://www.state.gov/r/pa/ei/bgn/2777.htm

Embassy

Embassy of Malaysia, Washington
3516 International Court, NW
Washington, DC 20008
Telephone: (202) 572-9700
Fax: (202) 572-9882
E-mail: malwashdc@kln.gov.my
URL: http://www.kln.gov.my/perwakilan/washington

2008 Malaysian ringgit—front (left); back (below)

Glossary

animists (AH-nih-mists)—People who believe that natural objects, such as rivers, rocks, and the wind, as well as plants and animals, have spirits.

Buddhist (BOO-dist)—A person who practices Buddhism, a Chinese religion practiced in many parts of the world.

Bumiputra (BOO-mee-POO-truh)—Malay "sons of the soil"—people whose ancestors lived in Malaysia or Indonesia.

char keoway teow (CHAR kway TEE-ow)—Fried flat noodles.

Christianity (KRIS-chee-AA-nih-tee)—A Western religion that teaches there is one God whose son Jesus is the savior (Christ).

cuisines (kwih-ZEENS)—Styles of cooking.

dhal (DOLL)—Sauce made with chick peas.

economy (ee-KAH-nuh-mee)—The flow of goods and money.

federation (feh-duh-RAY-shun)—A country's government.

Hindu (HIN-doo)—An Indian religion that recognizes several gods.

industry (IN-dus-tree)—A group of similar businesses.

Islam (IZ-lahm)—The religion of the Muslims that teaches there is one God, Allah, and that Mohammad is his prophet.

ketupat (keh-too-PAHT)—Rice boiled in small baskets of woven leaves.

laksa (LOK-sah)—Noodles served with fish curry sauce and other ingredients.

lemang (leh-MANG)—Sticky rice with coconut milk.

mee (MEE)—Noodles.

monsoon (mon-SOON)—A strong wind system that quickly changes direction and can bring heavy rain.

Muslim (MUZ-lim)—A person who practices the religion of Islam.

pandan (pan-DAN)—A kind of palm tree.

peninsula (peh-NIN-suh-luh)—A narrow strip of land that is almost completely surrounded by water.

rajah (RAH-jah)—A Malay or Indian prince.

Ramadan (RAH-mah-dahn)—The ninth month in the Muslim calendar, when Muslims do not eat during daylight hours.

rattan (rah-TAN)—A type of palm with long, tough stems that are used for making furniture and other things.

rendang (ren-DANG)—Meat cooked with spices and coconut milk.

roti canai (ROH-tee chah-NY)—Flatbread.

satay (sah-TAY)—Meat barbecued on skewers and served with a sauce made with coconut milk and peanuts.

sultan (SUL-tun)—A Muslim king.

trance (TRANTS)—A sleeplike state, when a person is not aware of what is going on in the usual way.

Index

ABOUT THE AUTHOR

Ann Weil has written many books for children, including *Meet Our New Student from Australia*, *Meet Our New Student from Tanzania*, and *Meet Our New Student from New Zealand* for Mitchell Lane Publishers. She is a world traveler and modern-day nomad. In the past fifteen years, she has lived in New York City, New Zealand, Australia, Austin (Texas), New Hampshire, and most recently in Westchester County, New York. She spent several months traveling in West

Malaysia, and stayed for some of that time with a Chinese Malaysian family in Penang. This photo of the author was taken in the Cameron Highlands of Malaysia in 1999.